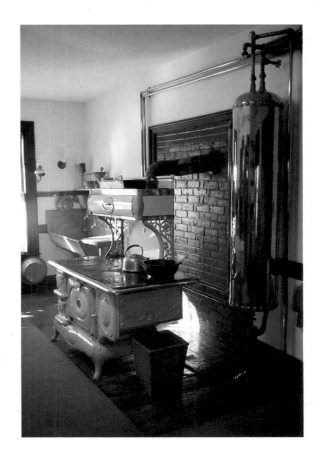

Brendan Gill and Dudley Witney

Summer Places

METHUEN

NEW YORK   LONDON   SYDNEY   TORONTO

FIRST AMERICAN EDITION
Published in the
United States of America by
Methuen, Inc.,
777 Third Avenue, New York,
N.Y. 10017
by arrangement with
McClelland and Stewart Limited,
Toronto, Ontario M4B 3G2,
Canada.

ISBN   0-458-93430-5
LCCCN 78-60954

PRINTED AND BOUND
IN THE U.S.A.

Designed by Frank Newfeld

Acknowledgments

We wish to thank the following for the help
and hospitality given to us on our travels:

Adirondack Museum

Mrs. Stephanie Barber

Mr. and Mrs. Frank E. Barnard

Mr. Frederick Beach

Mr. and Mrs. Hoff Benjamin

Mr. and Mrs. Richard Bortz

Mr. Campbell Boyd, Sr.

Mr. Paul Bransom

Mr. Robert Brown

Mr. and Mrs. Neil Bryson

Mr. William Canaday

Mrs. Clarke Case

Mr. William A. V. Cecil

Mr. and Mrs. Peter Cherniavsky

Mr. and Mrs. Sherman Chickering

Mr. and Mrs. Edward C. Childs

Mr. and Mrs. Rene Cira

Mr. and Mrs. James Clarke

Mr. and Mrs. Philip Clarke

Mr. and Mrs. Alan Comstock

Miss Susan Corlette

Mr. Peter Dominick

Mr. and Mrs. Laurence Edwards

Mrs. Lee Edwards

Mr. and Mrs. Tassos Fondaras

Mr. and Mrs. George Fuge

Mr. and Mrs. Richard Fulford

Mr. Anthony N. B. Garvan

Mr. Keith Gilborn

Miss Renée Graubart

Mrs. Melville Grosvenor

Dr. Chaton Haldipur

Mr. and Mrs. Ernest A. Hamill

Mr. Roy Hamilton

Mr. William Hamilton

Hearst Corporation

Mr. C. Wells Henderson

Mr. Harold Hochschild

Mr. and Mrs. Walter Hochschild

Mr. and Mrs. Robert Hohnstock

Dr. Denis Hopkins

Mr. Richard Horkins

Mr. Thomas Jones

Miss Sybil Kennedy

Mrs. Philae Knight

Mr. Fenwick Lansdowne

Miss Linda Lee

Dr. and Mrs. Maurice Lefford

Mr. Paul-Louis Martin

Mr. Sid Marty

Mr. and Mrs. Edward J. Mathews

Mrs. Arnold Matthews

Mrs. Elizabeth McClelland

Mr. Robert McClelland

Mr. and Mrs. Jim Miminos

Mr. Nick Miminos

Mr. Pat Morgan

Dr. and Mrs. Albert Moss

Mr. and Mrs. Robert Murray

Miss Hilda Neff

Mr. Toni Onley

Dr. and Mrs. Keith Palmer

Mr. Darraugh Park

Miss Susan Patterson

Mr. and Mrs. Anthony Quinton

Mrs. Joan Randall

Mr. and Mrs. Douglas Rice

Mr. and Mrs. Jeremy Riley

Mr. and Mrs. Maurice Roberts

The Rev. Walter Roberts

Miss Laura Rosen

Mrs. Constance Sanborn

Mr. John T. Sargent

Mr. Sean Scully

Mrs. Martha Shirer

Mr. Al Smith

Mrs. Mary Smith

Mr. Benjamin Sonnenberg

Mr. Jim Stephens

Miss Mary Alice Stewart

Mr. and Mrs. Ronald Sweet

Mr. Douglas Taplin

Dr. and Mrs. Oakley Thorne

Prof. Anderson Todd

Mrs. Barbara Toth

Dr. and Mrs. Evan Turner

Mr. and Mrs. John Walker

Mr. and Mrs. Michael Walker

Miss Jeannette Watson

Mr. and Mrs. Thomas J. Watson

Mr. Charles Wheaton

Mr. George M. White

Mr. Ronald Woodall

Mrs. James Young

Contents

For Anna

Summer Places

Summer places: to me the words are among the most haunting in the language. The sound of their mingled syllables seems to hint that something exceptionally pleasurable is just about to happen. All my life the words have been charged with the promise of wonders; they are charged also with the remembered promise of wonders that have long since occurred and that go on blazing in memory with an undiminished freshness. I have only to say "summer places" and I am pitched back at once into the bright greens and yellows of my earliest childhood; a happy, headlong journey and one that, no matter how often I am prompted to take it, holds welcome surprises.

It strikes me as curious that so much of my childhood should concern itself with summer. In our northerly climate, summer is but one of four seasons—a matter of a few delectable weeks of sun and flowering—and yet I doubt if I am alone in finding that my memories of summer are far more numerous, as well as far more vivid, than my memories of any other season. It is a time of adventure, of taking chances, of letting go. In summer places by the sea, the windows and doors of the big houses stand open to every breeze; sand drifts over the sills and thresholds, is grainy under one's bare feet on the boardwalks that march on rickety high stilts among the dunes. In the mountains, the air pours its invisible Niagaras through the tops of trees, making them sing, and at night fires burn and crumble on the stone hearths. Lying in bed at a window open to the stars, a child listens to the howling of a farmer's dog somewhere far down the valley and thinks with a shiver of contentment as he falls asleep, *Oh, greatest! I can hear a wolf.*

Unfailingly, summer places have been the agreeable ghosts that accompany me throughout the winter and help me to survive its bitter humors. They are robust and yet tender-hearted ghosts, not shadowy, unfeeling ones, and I hold out my hands to them for warmth. As I grow older, these ghosts of mine remain ever the same age, ever youthfully on tiptoe. It is morning with them; there is dew on the tops of the hedges among which they stand and somewhere far off a glint of sea.

Going back and back in time, I encounter the first of

my ghosts, a house we rented one summer on a curve of sandy shore looking out over Long Island Sound. It was a big, high-roofed, dark-red house, with many chimneys and dormer windows like dogs' heads barking out of every gable. The kitchen wing had been added onto again and again; one walked from kitchen to pantry to storeroom to porch to lean-to, in which bicycles, fish poles, and other summer gear were kept, and then on to the woodshed and latticed laundry yard, where, after a swim, the woolen bathing suits of those days would be hung on a clothes line to dry — which hour after hour, in spite of the sun, the suits refused to do. (At the time, children were forbidden to put on wet bathing suits because it was thought that their cold clamminess would chill the kidneys.)

I must have been three or four that year of the dark-red house, and for me the chief event of the summer was being allowed to stay up very late for the birthday party of a grown-up male member of the family. A bonfire burned on the lawn in his honor, lighting the undersides of the leaves of the maple trees rising all around it, and in the fiery dark the men attending the party were engaged in a game of tug-of-war. I was allowed to hold the slack end of the rope, in a safe position behind my stalwart father, the anchor man; and when, after a fierce struggle, his side won the contest, I was picked up and carried in triumph on his shoulders about the fire. Then everyone was singing, "The old gray mare, she ain't what she used to be, ain't what she used to be, *ain't* what she used to be..." and I was falling asleep in my mother's arms, not knowing what a mare was, feeling puzzled by the repeated "she"—the person for whom the party was being given was obviously a "he"—and feeling still more puzzled by the word "ain't." It was a word heard in the kitchen, not a word ever to be used by me; yet there it was, being mysteriously bawled aloud by my parents and uncles and aunts and cousins, in the summer night under all those stars.

My second ghost is a house that my parents built a year or so later, in the same little town on the Connecticut shore. The roads of that town were of tar that year after year had been poured out in successive thin layers over the age-old sand of the district; and on exceptionally hot days the tar would melt and the surface of the roads would erupt in tiny, cone-shaped islands of sand, out of which to my astonishment ants would emerge and go about their business. Impossible to walk barefoot on the hot tar; making one's way to the local ice cream and candy store, one leapt heroically from sandy island to island. An electric trolley line ran through the woods on a narrow right-of-way a couple of hundred yards from our house. Almost silent and yet very powerful, the open summer trolleys, with their varnished oak and mahogany seats and shiny brass fittings, rocked along at high speed through foliage that, as one leaned recklessly out from the wooden running boards, brushed in a green blur against one's cheeks and half-shut eyes.

Throughout the summer the family would make excursions by trolley to a nearby amusement park called Savin Rock. (The name was always pronounced Seven Rock, and again I experienced a child's difficulty with the waywardness of language: why wasn't "rock" in the plural if there were seven of them?) At Savin Rock were flying horses and a roller-coaster and something called Snap-the-Whip and an Old Red Mill, through whose winding, water-filled passageways one floated in tubs, in total darkness, until, rounding a bend, one would suddenly come upon a hideous, dangling skeleton. Little girls would scream and little boys would bite their lips and utter never a sound. And in a sideshow at Savin Rock was a black man in an iron cage, billed as "The Wild Man of Borneo." He was naked except for a length of mangy leopard skin about his black loins, and from time to time he would jump to his feet, rattle the bars of his cage, and shout some incomprehensible mumbo-jumbo. Years later I learned that he was one of a number of shiftless, hard-drinking gardeners whom the summer people regularly hired and no less regularly fired between June and September. He found sitting idle in a cage in a tent more pleasant than mowing lawns and weeding flower beds out under a blazing sun. Moreover, he liked shouting, because the more he shouted the more Irish whiskey would be doled out to him after work by the impresario of the sideshow. One day my father on an impulse climbed up onto the platform beside the cage. A handsome, blue-eyed man of commanding presence, he was dressed all in white, with a jaunty straw boater upon his head. He was already a well-known physician and surgeon in Connecticut and many people in the crowd immediately recognized him. He took a cardboard megaphone from the sideshow barker and announced that he had just completed a thorough examination of the Wild Man of Borneo, that he was happy to vouch for the fact that the Wild Man was indeed the genuine article, and that the Wild Man embodied an astonishing throwback in human physiology covering a period of well over fifty thousand years. Upon which the Wild Man, who had often been hired and fired by my father, jumped to his feet, rattled the bars of his cage, and shouted, "Jameson! Jameson!" in what seemed to the crowd an authentically ferocious

Borneo-ese accent. Oh, but I was proud of my father that day!

The new house that my parents built was larger and sturdier than most of the cottages in town. It was a house that one could have lived in comfortably in winter, with a big living room paneled in chestnut and a screened porch full of the latest fashion in wicker chairs and sofas, which (wonderful to a child) went on whispering to one another for a long time after people had got up and walked away. Upstairs there were several bedrooms, each painted a different color, and a sleeping porch open on three sides, containing a row of white-painted iron cots, one per child. The third floor of the house was an open attic, stiflingly hot by day and slow to cool at night. The pine roofers overhead and the planks of the floor were of new lumber, which oozed a gummy sap as the temperature rose. For us, who moved on to other summer places, that attic was never to be the treasure house of cast-off clothing and abandoned furniture that most family attics become; of its scanty contents, I recall only a few dozen brightly colored Japanese lanterns left over from a gala housewarming.

The night of the housewarming, we children were all abed on the sleeping porch. Guests had been invited to come to the party in costume, and one of the guests, an old friend of the family, came out to say hello to us, where we lay listening in the dark. He was dressed as Pierrot, in black-and-white silk lozenges from head to foot, and he wore a white mask. As he bent over my sister's cot to give her a good-night kiss, he took off his mask and at first all that she could see of him was an immense, bristling black mustache. She shrieked and burst into tears as the embarrassed guest hurried away. An orchestra was playing on the ground floor, so no one could hear her crying; no one would come to console her. "Sissy!" I called from my nearby cot, eager to enhance her misery. "Sissy, sissy, sissy!"

All summer, we lay on the porch at night, striving to stay awake long enough to share in a certain marvelous event: at ten o'clock, far out on the Sound, the night boat traveling between New York and Hartford would turn the beam of its searchlight inward from the Sound to seek out our house on the shore. The captain of the boat was a patient of my father's, and his daily bathing of our house with light was a seafaring man's way of paying homage. We would stare up at the varnished matchwood ceiling of the porch, all inky black one moment and the next as bright as day; still another moment, and the beam would swing off skyward, avoiding our neighbors' houses, and the dark would come rushing back in over us. How could one doubt the good fortune of a family in which such things were possible?

Childhood and summertime have much in common, but childhood passes and whether we welcome it or not our summers are transformed; the wonders when they come are wonders of a different kind. The mercy of memory lies in letting us keep what we have lost. I have before my eyes after fifty years the brown dancing bear that, chained to his keeper, strolled once a summer on his hind legs through the town, holding out a tambourine for coins; the Italian organ-grinder and his capering monkey, dressed in red and gold; and those bad-tempered, scolding creatures—parrots, ponies, and peacocks—that we admired but kept a wary distance from.

Sooner perhaps than we are ready for it, we pass from being children to being parents of children, heads of households, builders and preservers of summer places for the next rung in the ever-lengthening ladder of generations. The woodland paths that my children and grandchildren labor to keep open in summer were blazed and cleared upwards of a hundred years ago by one of their great-great-grandfathers. The lake where they swim was a favorite retreat of his; here he would ride his horse on a Sunday morning, dismount, undress among the laurels on the shore, take a long swim (his horse swimming along beside him), then jump up onto the bank, dry himself, dress, and ride back into town in time for church—a grave, white-bearded man wearing his best black Sunday suit. The church, like the lake, is just as it used to be, and so is the old clapboard house in which he lived and the maple four-poster in which he slept.

When, at some midsummer family festival, we raise our glasses and propose our traditional toast—"To our beloved absent ones, wherever they may be!"—we are drinking to the dead as well as to the living; and they seem, that innumerable host, to crowd all round us on such occasions.

One then begins to approach, however tentatively, an explanation of the mystery of why the fleeting summers of our childhood claim such a large share of our memories. May it not be because more of the fabric of family affection is woven in summer than in any other season? When we are at our summer places, are we not more open to ourselves and to one another than we would otherwise be? Are we not readier then to risk the give-and-take by which ordinary family affection may be hammered into family love? There is something at work upon us during those long summer days, drawing us close, making us happy in our closeness. Walk the shaded verandah—surely it is there at the next turning. Or surely it is in the gazebo on the rocky height above the river, or beyond the open bedroom window where at twilight the white muslin curtains blow inward. Whatever it may be, it draws us on and we are glad to follow.

Summer Places

WHEN the first shiploads of settlers reached the North American continent in the seventeenth century, the wilderness began at the very shores off which they dropped anchor. A short stretch of sand, rock, and brambles, and then they faced what must have seemed to them an impenetrable forest extending no man knew how far westward. In the event, it turned out that the forest was easier to penetrate than it appeared; trees were girdled and burned, or chopped down for lumber and fuel, and tilled fields and pastures were laid bare to the sun. The climate was a surprise and a disappointment, being hotter in summer and colder in winter than the climate they had been accustomed to in the Old World. But they shouldered that burden without much protest—it wasn't, after all, in pursuit of fine weather that they had sailed in their cockleshell ships week after week across the inimical Atlantic. Moreover, extremes of nature were manifestations of God's mysterious goodness; what couldn't be admired in His handiwork must be borne with resignation. "God's will be done" embraced flood, drought, fire, ice, and pestilence.

By the late eighteenth century, in the broad, gently rising sweep of land between the Atlantic and the wrinkled, ancient Appalachian range, there were hundreds of thousands of acres of flourishing farmland and thousands of prosperous villages and towns. There were even a few large cities, in which could be found wealthy individuals eager to avoid, in the hot seasons, the stench and noise and recurrent maladies of urban life. With astonishing speed, the lonely wilderness that had struck terror into the heart of the first English, French, and Spanish adventurers became a source of inspiration to their descendants. In a mere handful of generations, men went from fearing solitude to seeking it; having built cities as crowded and uncomfortable and disease-ridden as those they had left behind in Europe, they cast about for a means of escaping them. And so the first summer places came into existence. Sometimes they were called retreats and sometimes they were called pavilions, and nearly always they had it in common that they pretended to be simpler and closer to nature than they really were. What they shared above all was a certain intention, which translated itself into a certain tone: they were to be both carefree and health-giving.

From the start the link with health was a crucial one.

Frivolous social occasions were frowned on, especially in New England and among the Quakers to the south; but if a social occasion was seen to be based on a man's need to restore his health, plainly that was a different matter. In this respect, the colonists were able to follow an example set for them in the New World as well as in the Old. In Europe people with the means to do so had been taking the waters for centuries, not to say millennia. The city of Bath, in England, was a fashionable watering place in the 1700s, and it had been no less fashionable among the Romans living in England some fifteen hundred years earlier. Bath boasts the only hot mineral springs in the British Isles; but there are scores of mineral springs on the continent, both hot and cold, around which fashionable resorts have been developing for centuries. The German word *"Bad"* means both "bath" and "watering place" and is part of hundreds of German place-names. Baden-Baden, for example, was the official bathing station for the Roman legions quartered in what is now Strasbourg and, in the time of Marcus Aurelius, was a thriving outpost of the Roman Empire. One can therefore say of it without exaggeration that it has been a popular resort for upwards of two thousands years. Spa, in Belgium, was so well thought of by wealthy eighteenth-century travelers enjoying a cure there that the name of the town quickly became, in English, a lower-case noun.

If taking the waters was a commonplace in Europe, it was also a commonplace in North America. For countless generations before the white man arrived, Indians had made it a practice to visit mineral springs and, in summer, to set up encampments by them. It is commonly held that the first town in the American colonies to become a popular summer resort was Stafford Springs, in the sandy eastern reaches of Connecticut, and its popularity in the early eighteenth century was based on the reputation of its mineral springs. The Indians in that vicinity had generously called the springs to the attention of the settlers trudging down into the Connecticut forest from the Massachusetts Bay Colony a hundred years earlier; soon these settlers returned the Indians' kindness by shouldering them aside and asserting possession of the springs, which remained an attraction to "society" until well into the nineteenth century. Further to the south were Yellow Springs and Bath Springs, both in Pennsylvania, which claim to date back to the 1720s. The innumerable springs of the Virginias, of which Hot Springs and White Sulphur Springs are probably the best known, became popular by the middle of the eighteenth century, as did Saratoga Springs, in New York State, and Poland Springs, in Maine. Hundreds

Saratoga, New York

Interior of men's bathhouse, Warm Springs, Virginia

Exterior of men's bathhouse, Warm Springs, Virginia

Gazebo, Chester Springs, Pennsylvania

Warm Springs, Virginia

Chester Springs, Pennsylvania

Shelter for drinking fountain
Warm Springs, Virginia

Saratoga, New York

and perhaps thousands of cities, towns, and villages scattered throughout the fifty states bear "Springs" as a portion of their names; there are even a few towns content to be known solely as "Springs." In most cases, these springs are not mineral and do not pretend to promote health; having an abundance of fresh water for drinking and cooking purposes, they were convenient sites to settle by.

Mineral springs vied with each other in boasting not only that they would help to preserve the health of visitors but that they were capable of curing an astounding variety of ailments, interior and exterior. Washington visited his brother Lawrence at Berkeley Springs, in Virginia, when Lawrence was dying there of tuberculosis. Like many other mortally ill people in that period, he had gone to the springs in the vain hope of being saved. Ironically, it must often have been the case that people in good health who made a practice of visiting spas would contract in the course of these visits some of the very diseases they were bent on avoiding; for in the days before germs were known to exist, nobody hesitated to bathe with invalids and drink with them from the same common tin cup.

Resorts that owed their existence to the pursuit of health tended to encourage religion and temperance as well. If one wished to be strengthened both physically and spiritually, an obvious means was much heartfelt hymn-singing and penitence, unaccompanied by alcohol. Little by little, however, thoughts of an abstinent hereafter gave way to a concern for things of a happier, more down-to-earth nature, such as party-going, party-giving, match-making, horse-racing, and gambling. In town after town, racetracks and casinos—known to their enemies as gambling hells—rose within sight of the local medicinal springs, giving visitors an immediate choice of very different recreations. In Saratoga, for example, Richard Canfield's famous gambling house (now preserved as a museum and civic center) stands only a few yards away from the Congress Spring, the most popular of the town's early springs: Sodom and Gomorrah serenely confronting Hygeia.

Throughout the nineteenth century, as the population of the country doubled and tripled and as the national wealth increased at a rate even greater than that of the population, real estate speculators began to seek out advantageous sites for summer resorts from coast to coast and from the lakes and forests of Canada to the beaches of the Gulf of Mexico. In the hot summers characteristic of the North American continent, one could escape the fiery cauldrons of cities only by a laborious journey into the mountains or to some breezy shore, whether of lake or river or ocean.

This late in the twentieth century, it is hard for us to recollect how much effort our ancestors had to devote to outwitting heat. For us the now commonplace miracle of air-conditioning makes it possible to achieve whatever climate we like by merely fiddling with a set of dials. Even without air-conditioning, we can mitigate the fierceness of our summers by dressing scantily and eating prudently. In the nineteenth century, people wore nearly as much clothing in summer as they did in winter; and in any season, there were layers of suffocating undergarments to contend with, especially for women; fresh air, to say nothing of sunlight, was rarely allowed to reach the bare skin. As for meals, they were murderously ample, both winter and summer: thick soups, meat, fish, breads, pies, cakes, and ice cream, with boxes of chocolates and other candy always at hand. By the time prosperous middle-class men and women were in their thirties, they were beginning to be overweight; by their forties, they were often dangerously corpulent. No wonder that, after a big luncheon or dinner, they were content to sit semi-comatose on the verandahs of summer houses or summer hotels, listlessly fanning themselves or, more wisely, retiring to their rooms for a nap while the prolonged act of digestion took place. Except for the young and slender, strenuous exercise was out of the question; one might go so far as to undertake a carriage ride through the green countryside or along the shore, but even a dip in the sea required an effort that to many vacationers seemed not worth making. Better to drowse in peace than to risk sunstroke and drowning!

The location of one's summer place depended primarily on the means of transportation available. As these means changed from decade to decade, so did the sites on which people found it desirable to build summer cottages. Because travel by water was the cheapest and most convenient method of transportation in the eighteenth and early nineteenth centuries, a large number of summer resorts grew up around such readily accessible seaports as Newport, Rhode Island, Portsmouth, New Hampshire, and Portland, Maine. Even in the days of sail, Charleston ship-owners, merchants, and planters had close commercial ties with Newport and so they were among the first to settle their families there in summer, at a safe distance from the sultry, malarial climate they confronted at home.

While some antebellum Charlestonians were summering at Newport, others were settling in a summer place that, though far less distant, was far more uncomfortable to reach: they traveled on horseback and by coach across South Carolina to the foothills of the Blue Ridge, where on a 2,000-foot-high plateau at Flat Rock, North Carolina (a favorite gathering place of the Cherokee Nation in ancient times), they founded in the 1820s a colony that many of their descendants continue to frequent today. The wealthy lowland settlers brought with them a small army of slaves, who helped clear the land and build substantial houses; soon an Episcopal church was constructed and given the appropriate name of St. Mary in the Wilderness. The district came to be known as "The Little Charleston of the Mountains"; and with balls and much visiting back and forth, every effort was made to imitate the mode of life of English country gentlemen. Not that business was altogether forgotten. Many of the settlers were bankers and they were well aware that, aside from its salubrious climate, Flat Rock was on the route of a highway that would some day link the states opening up beyond the Great Smokies—Tennessee, Kentucky, and the like—with the eastern seaboard. Over that road would pass the garnered wealth of the interior and ideally its terminus would prove to be Charleston.

In the event, the dreamed-of highway yielded to a dreamed-of railroad, the building of which was long postponed because of the Civil War and its aftermath. When, in the 1880s, railroad lines were at last being pushed through the high valleys of the Smokies, Flat Rock was considered to be of little importance; commerce had passed it by. Thus, to its good fortune, it remains today very like what it was a hundred and fifty years ago—a small summer resort hidden away in a cool green mountain forest.

The coming of steam transportation, first manifested in ships, brought a notable increase in speed of travel and in the reliability of scheduled times of arrival and departure. These were both important factors in the increasing popularity of a nineteenth-century innovation: summer vacations, to be taken and enjoyed not merely by school children but by prosperous middle-class working adults as well. Having plenty of leisure, the rich had always been able to accommodate themselves readily to the vagaries of sail and stagecoach, but most people had jobs to attend to and were obliged to follow strict schedules. Moreover, in the nineteenth century one customarily worked six days a week; to gain the advantage of a two-day weekend required much juggling of timetables. (Looking back from the 1970s, we are startled to observe how much at the mercy of timetables our ancestors were; it wasn't until the automobile became a common form of transporta-

tion that people were free to come and go as they pleased).

Public transportation held little attraction for the very rich, who preferred making their way in their own luxurious steam yachts to such exclusive landfalls as Bar Harbor, Murray Bay, and the Thousand Islands. As for the ordinary vacationer, he depended on one or another of the hundreds of steamship lines that kept boats running punctually up and down the Atlantic coast and its adjacent rivers, from the St. John, in Florida, to the St. Lawrence. On the Gulf of Mexico, steamers carried passengers to summer places at Point Clear, Biloxi, Ocean Springs, and Pass Christian. Other steamers, with their immense, clattering paddle wheels, churned the waters of Lake Pontchartrain, carrying passengers away from the heat and fever of New Orleans to sleepy inland towns like Mandeville and Covington, sheltered by ancient forest trees and cooled by breezes off the lake. By the turn of the twentieth century, there can scarcely have been a sizeable body of water anywhere on the continent that didn't boast at least one small, white-painted steamer proudly afloat on it—a steamer that in many cases would have been hauled in sections long distances overland and assembled on the spot by men who might hitherto never have seen a boat.

Of the intricate network of steamship lines that once provided water transport for vacationers from coast to coast, nearly all have vanished without a trace. Only a few score ferries remain, serving those islands—Prince Edward Island, Newfoundland, Martha's Vineyard, Nantucket, Catalina, and the like—that lie unbridgeably far from the mainland.

The curious bond between summer places and religion continued to strengthen throughout most of the nineteenth century. God provided the occasion for the founding of summer colonies and Mammon turned the colonies into an occasion for profitable real estate development. Faithfully every summer, thousands of religious enthusiasts traveled by steamer to the Methodist camp meeting held at Oak Bluffs, on Martha's Vineyard. There, at first in dormitory tents strewn with hay for sleeping and later in snug little wooden cottages with pretty jig-saw Gothic decoration, "the days of prayer and meditation" were transformed into "seasons of elaboration and bustle." (Such, at any rate, was the disapproving observation of a journalist writing about Oak Bluffs in the 1860s.)

Other celebrated camp meetings were held at sites along the New Jersey shore and along the shores of The Great Lakes. Gradually the religious groups mingled their purposes with those of the non-sectarian "Chautauqua movement," which was founded in a

Lake Joseph, Ontario

Oak Bluffs, Massachusetts

Church at Oak Bluffs, Massachusetts

grove on the shores of Lake Chautauqua, in upper New York State, just over a hundred years ago, and quickly spread throughout the country. Chautauquas placed strong emphasis upon plain living and high thinking; lectures were given by learned figures, prayer and song were encouraged, and alcohol was, of course, forbidden. The fashionable summer resort of Point O'Woods, on Fire Island, New York, was once a Chautauqua colony; to this day, if liquor were to be sold at Point O'Woods, title would revert to the original owners.

The coming of railroads had an even more profound effect on the siting of summer places than the coming of steamships had had in an earlier generation. Many locations of great natural beauty that were far from any navigable body of water proved easily accessible by train. Hitherto impenetrable mountain ranges opened up in the course of laying the rails that would eventually span the continent. On a smaller scale, railroads that came into being in order to serve cities within a comparatively close range of one another (The New York, New Haven and Hartford Railroad, for example) made available for profitable real estate development dozens of picturesque villages along their rights-of-way.

The religious colonists were quick to adjust themselves to the new technology; they saw that railroads would be useful to them and that they would be useful to railroads. An organization called the Methodist State Camp Ground Association hit upon a likely site for a summer encampment on the eastern shore of Lake Michigan, not far from the small city of Petosky. The Association took care to interest the Grand Rapids and Indiana Railway Company in the project; and the Company, foreseeing a large increase in passenger traffic on the Petosky branch, offered what newspapers of the day referred to as "valuable donations of land and money." (Railroad companies always had plenty of land at their disposal; it was money that they were reluctant to give away.) The trustees of the Methodist State Camp Ground Association, reporting on the site of the village that would one day be Bay View, wrote in part:

> It is accessible alike to the Upper and Lower Peninsulas. It is at the head of the inland navigation route, through Burt and Mullet lakes to Cheboygan, which offers superior advantages to the excursionists. It is on one of the most beautiful bodies of water in the country. It falls properly within the Mackinaw region, which must be through all time the great summer resort of the northwest. It is

directly on the line of the Grand Rapids and Indiana Railroad, which has extensive connections with many other leading railroad lines throughout the State and country. Petosky can therefore be reached by boat or rail from all points, south and east, with the greatest ease. Tickets can be purchased in all the principal cities of the country, which will carry the passengers directly to the camp ground, a fact which can be stated of no other camp ground in America. The region of Petosky is known to be a *Sanitarium* for hay fever, asthma, and catarrhal affections, while the whole country for scores of miles in almost every direction offers facilities for recreation which are simply endless.

Few advertising men could have outdone those Methodist men of God when it came to writing seductive promotion copy. The village of Bay View was founded within a few months of the publication of their report and in 1975 it celebrated its one hundredth birthday.

Almost from the beginning the railroads were aware that they could greatly increase passenger traffic, especially over long distances and in thinly populated areas, by building resort hotels in scenic settings adjacent to their tracks. Surveyors laying out rights-of-way were instructed to keep an eye peeled for likely situations, which ideally would include a lofty view, a lake, a waterfall, or a mineral spring. Architects were encouraged to devise hotels that were romantic confections of stone, wood, and glass, all the more astonishing in their luxury because of their unexpectedness.

Perhaps the most startling example of how to invent a popular resort overnight by means of skillful public relations was the Canadian Pacific Railway Company's ingenious exploitation of the beauty—and intimidating isolation—of the Canadian Rockies. The company had gained political and financial backing in large measure because the young Dominion needed to forge a visible link between east and farthest west; but the expense of building a railroad over arduous mountain terrain, long stretches of which contained no sources of revenue from either freight or passengers, threatened to bankrupt the company. (A measure of the boldness of the undertaking is the fact that when the Canadian Pacific set out to build its line across the continent, Canada had a population of around four million people; when the United States built its first transcontinental line, it had a population of forty million.) William Cornelius Van

Railroad station, Banff, Alberta

Horne, the man in charge of driving the line through the Rockies, made an epigram out of his difficulties: "We can't export the scenery—we'll import the tourists!"

And this the vigorous, ebullient Van Horne proceeded to do. As Esther Fraser tells the story in her book, *The Canadian Rockies,* in the 1880s Van Horne lured scores of artists, writers, and photographers into the Rockies and prompted them to spread word of the district's Alpine beauty. Though up to that time nobody had ever been known to play among those lonely peaks, Van Horne didn't hesitate to describe them in elaborate brochures as "The Mountain Playground of the World." Posters on billboards throughout the world boasted of "Parisian Politeness on the Canadian Pacific," and the Canadian Pacific trains were indeed among the most deluxe in existence. In a spectacular location once humbly known as Siding 29 and wisely renamed Banff Springs (a mineral spring had fortunately been discovered in the neighborhood), the celebrated New York architect Bruce Price was commissioned to design a vast hotel in a vaguely French style, high on the slopes of Sulphur Mountain; soon Van Horne was advertising it as "The Finest Hotel on the North American Continent." Whether the claim was true or false—and it was certainly closer to true than to false—it had its intended effect; thousands of trippers poured into Banff Springs and later, under the same prodding of superlatives, into Lake Louise and Jasper Park.

With a rapidity that owed less to good business sense than to a speculative fever not unlike that of the South Sea Bubble, railroads wove an ever more complicated cat's cradle of tracks across the continent. Millions of acres of open country and wilderness, whether in the Maritime Provinces, the Adirondacks, the Far West, or along the Big Sur, were made accessible to the public for the first time. A cult of the forest sprang up among the very rich. At the same moment and with the same unprecedented extravagance, Pierre Lorillard was building his 7,000-acre Tuxedo Park in the Ramapo Mountains, George Vanderbilt was building Biltmore House in the Great Smokies—easily the biggest and most attractive country house ever built in America, set in an estate of well over a hundred thousand acres—and the promoter William West Durant was preparing in the Adirondacks a series of playfully rustic "camps" for the Morgans, Vanderbilts, and Huntingtons, while out on the West Coast the Hearsts were accumulating the land that would eventually provide the ten-mile-long Pacific shoreline of San Simeon.

In a guidebook, *The Northern Lakes of Canada,* published in the 1880s, the author entitles his opening chapter "A Little Farther On," and begins at once to chide his readers:

> It may fairly be said that there is scarcely a tourist who lands on the shores of America, who does not visit Niagara Falls, and there are thousands of inhabitants of this Continent who feel impelled to follow their example.
>
> Not to have seen Niagara in these days of rapid communication, is to admit one's self to be behind the age, therefore, it is, that as in Europe, the old saying is, "All the roads lead to Rome," so on this continent all the routes lead to Niagara Falls, and everybody can go there if they will.
>
> The object of this little sketch may be frankly avowed to be that when the visitor shall have reached Niagara, it may, by telling him truthfully what there is beyond, encourage him to come a *little farther on* . . . into the interior of the country, to "The Northern Lakes of Canada," where primeval forests jostle close with summer hotels, and nature can be studied and enjoyed, freed from the artificialities of every-day city life.

The author is especially eloquent on the subject of the Lakes of Muskoka, in the Highlands of Ontario, north of Toronto:

> . . . a region of many, many lakes of all sizes and forms, where canoeing and boating from hamlet to hamlet along the shores, combines the safety of a scattered population with the wilderness of uncultivated wastes. This is no matter of choice or taste with the hardy settler, for nature has so accumulated the rocks and wild along the shores that only at intervening spots can sufficient breadth of soil be found on which to farm. The hotels are not great caravansaries, but moderate houses where plain meals, fresh milk, cleanly rooms and *comfortable* as distinguished from *elegant* accompaniments, are joined with *moderate* as distinguished from *high-priced* charges.

As the book proceeds, the italics multiply, for like Van Horne of the Canadian Pacific, the author is an evangelist. (He is also, not by coincidence, passenger agent for the Northern and Northwestern Railway, "the great and only line running to the far-famed Muskoka District.")

Throughout the 1890s and well past the turn of the twentieth century, the lakes of the Muskoka country — Lake Muskoka itself, Lake Rosseau, and Lake Joseph—enjoyed boom times. Many who came as tourists decided to establish summer places there;

hundreds of shingle-and-stone cottages, with attendant docks and boathouses, emerged along their wooded shores. A large proportion of the new settlers were wealthy Americans, some of them from New York and, surprisingly, a greater number from Pittsburgh. A glance at a railroad map of the time makes the reason clear: by rail it was far simpler to get from Pittsburgh to the Muskoka lakes than to get to summer resorts along the New England coast.

As long as railroads were the primary means of transportation on the continent, summer places were likely to spring up in their vicinity. This likelihood was not without drawbacks. For example, when the Adirondack Railroad was first contemplated, back in the 1860s, the *New York Times* commented, "Within an easy day's ride of our great city, as steam teaches us to measure distance, is a tract of country fitted to make a Central Park for the world...[With completion of the railroad] the Adirondack region will become a suburb of New York." Fortunately for the Adirondacks, the *Times*'s prophecy was radically optimistic, but it was nevertheless the case that by 1900 there were few corners of the continent, however remote, that hadn't come within reach of rail and hence hadn't been threatened with a popularity that might destroy them.

First ships, then trains, and then automobiles. It was thought that the automobile, having begun as a toy of the very rich, would remain inaccessibly expensive, requiring along with its initial high cost a chauffeur to keep it in order and drive it; but by dint of mass-production and a series of inventions such as the electric self-starter, it soon became both comparatively cheap to buy and maintain and comparatively easy to handle. By the 1920s, it was a customary adjunct of middle-class life and, at least in America, was beginning to prove indispensable to the blue-collar worker as well. (A sign of this change was the gradual supplanting of the patrician word "automobile" by the plebian word "car.") For the first time in history, millions of people were free to travel ad lib, over distances long or short, without consulting timetables or purchasing tickets. On a whim they could take to the open road, which as the years passed was transformed at public expense into a network of highways far more complex than the earlier network of railroad lines had been.

As the leisure time of the working classes increased, so did their capacity to take advantage of it. Sports, travel, and other pastimes hitherto reserved to the wealthy were eagerly adopted by small shopkeepers and artisans. In Canada, as in the United States, immense stretches of empty land were for sale cheap, which wave after wave of a new kind of summer people came to colonize. Not for them a chateau in the Great Smokies, exquisitely imitating Blois and Amboise, or an Italianate palazzo in Newport, grander than the original by which it was inspired. The new summer people built cozy cottages—sometimes, indeed, they were only shanties—that stood herded together on narrow plots, and not simply because the purchasers of the properties were people of small means and could afford nothing grander but also because they were city-dwellers, accustomed to and enjoying close contact with their neighbors. In their newly acquired summer places, they fished and swam and sunbathed within a few feet of one another, and felt content to be doing so because solitude held a hint of menace to them. Their hearts quailed at the thought of being surrounded by a limitless, unpopulated expanse of field or forest; they liked looking out at night and seeing through a nearby scrim of trees a lighted window. Whatever else the darkness might contain, there lay safety.

The democratization of summer places is a continuing phenomenon of the twentieth century—so much so that people begin to speak less and less of summer places and more and more of second homes. With prosperity comes multiplicity: if one is good, surely two is better? Still, the difference in nomenclature is profound, a second house implying something on the order of importance of a second car or a second topcoat. The new phrase doesn't evoke the image, charged with romance, of a sanctuary to which one journeys in order to escape both the heat of summer and the burden of winter's responsibilities. That kind of sanctuary still exists, and so does solitude, but at a price.

To be truly isolated nowadays one must seek out areas unapproachable by train or car, and just here we encounter the fourth great revolution in methods of transportation: flight. If one is rich enough to own a private plane, then one has the pick of a thousand, or ten thousand, remote sites: a scatteration of rocky islands in Georgian Bay, a box canyon in New Mexico, green with willows, a pocket handkerchief of pasture somewhere in the High Sierras. Even on commercial flights, new summer places have come within easy reach of the traveler. By air from New York, one is no farther today from a ranch in Wyoming than, a hundred years ago, one would have been from a camp in the Catskills. Measured in hours, the distance between Toronto and Vancouver amounts to what was once the distance between Toronto and Ottawa. For the traveler, the world shrinks and his choice of destinations expands.

The Gulf Coast

The Gulf of Mexico is unjustly diminished by its name: it is not so much a gulf as an immense sea, stretching a thousand miles from east to west and some fifteen hundred miles from north to south. Its North American shoreline, running in a great loop from Key West, Florida, to Brownsville, Texas, at the Mexican border, is almost seventeen hundred miles long. Moreover, the Gulf reaches well into the heartland of the continent; much of it lies west of Tulsa, Topeka, and Winnipeg. The Mississippi River pours into the Gulf at the rate of 600,000 cubic feet of water a second and the Gulf Stream pours out of it with such force that, crossing the North Atlantic, it embraces the far-off coast of Ireland, bringing to the climate of that northern island, which would otherwise be as cold as Labrador, a warmth that permits palms and other tropic flora to prosper.

The broad, gently sloping, white-sand beaches of the Gulf amount to an enormous marine playground, miles of which remain benignly unbuilt-upon. And this is surprising, because visitors from the North have been traveling to the Gulf Coast in all seasons for a couple of centuries now, in summer seeking its cool breezes, in winter its hot sun. When the weather is fine, the Coast has the quiet—perhaps even the lassitude—of some long-extended dream, but its smiling aspects can be deceptive; the Gulf is the source of some of the fiercest storms that afflict the earth. In Galveston, for example, in September, 1900, a hurricane and flood all but destroyed the city and took a toll of some five thousand lives. Again and again, resorts along the Coast have been smashed to smithereens by the power of wind and water. In some places, the wrecked resorts have been rebuilt; in others, nothing remains but an occasional broken seawall, or a brick pier rising out of the eelgrass and beach plum that have usurped the old mossy lawns of some once-flourishing community.

Most of the houses along the Gulf are
raised high on brick piers or wooden
piles, partly to induce, by convection,
cool breezes under the first floor and
partly to outwit the flooding that accom-
panies the repeated violent hurricanes
and winter storms of the region.

On the beach at Galveston: the sand is
so hard that it is readily driven upon,
serving as an informal highway for beach
buggies and other vehicles. Since there
are no private beaches in Texas, they
become in summer immense outdoor living-
rooms, crowded where access to them is
easy but for many miles as empty as they
must have been when the first Spanish and
French explorers set foot on them.

Overleaf, a Victorian grape arbor in
Covington, Louisiana, and some charac-
teristically intricate jigsaw work on a
verandah in Mandeville, Louisiana. The
pierced brackets, larger than need be,
help to soften the fierce summer light.

Left, a pathway at Point Clear, Alabama. During the Battle of Mobile Bay, in the Civil War, Admiral Farragut of the Union Navy ordered Point Clear to be fired on; a cannonball shattered the wall of a house behind the picket fence. *Below,* a house in Mandeville. *At bottom,* a view of Lake Pontchartrain.

A riverside house in Covington. In the early days, summer
places were reached mostly by water; from New Orleans, people
journeyed in paddle-wheel steamers out to the comparatively
fever-free villages along the Gulf or up-country. There was
little thought then of sporting activity in summer: one sat in
the shade of a wide gallery, stirring the air with a palmetto
fan and watching the sun fall slowly into distant treetops.

More on sporting activity at the turn of the century:
for many, it was sufficient exercise to rock back
and forth on a swing like this, fashioned in Covington.
In the design of houses, climate is more important
even than fashion. Though different in style, the houses
shown here are equally bent on controlling sunlight and
furnishing ample cross-ventilation for their occupants.

Left
A shell shop in Galveston.
People come from all over
the world to collect shells
on the beaches of the Gulf,
from Brownsville, Texas,
to Key West, Florida.
Lovers of shells rarely
show any interest in
swimming or sunbathing;
they walk face downward,
like monks in prayer.

Right
A powerboat securely
moored in air. Owners of
true sailing craft regard
the ubiquitous "stink-pot"
with derision, asserting that
many powerboat owners
steer a course by means
of Exxon road maps.

Overleaf
A pier running out into
the Gulf at Pass Christian.
The beach falls away so
gradually that one may
be hundreds of yards
at sea and not yet beyond
one's depth.

The Blue Ridge

The Appalachians are the oldest mountain range on earth. The glaciers of several ice ages have scoured away their sharp edges, reduced their height, and filled their valleys with innumerable lakes and streams. The Appalachians comprise several mountain systems bearing different names —the Laurentians, the Adirondacks, the Berkshires, the Alleghenies, and the like. The mountains known collectively as the Blue Ridge run across Virginia into North Carolina, where they mingle to the west with the Great Smokies and, to the south, peter out in the foothills of Georgia. The highest peak east of the Mississippi is Mount Mitchell, in the Blue Ridge, which rises to a height of just over six thousand feet. For well over a hundred years, the high plateaux of this mountain country have been a favorite summer resort for well-to-do southerners seeking escape from the suffocating heat of the lowlands. The chief city of the district is Asheville. Once it had become accessible by rail, in the 1880s, it developed into a resort for northerners as well as southerners. Moreover, because at the time it was thought that fresh mountain air would help to cure tuberculosis, victims of that disease came to Asheville and its environs from all over the world. So cosmopolitan did Asheville consider itself by the turn of the century that a local writer described it as "the Paris of North Carolina"—a compliment smaller than the writer may have supposed it to be. Still, it was true that Sarah Bernhardt and many other European celebrities performed in Asheville and that "society" also visited there and, in the case of George Vanderbilt and others, found the climate and scenery sufficiently attractive to set up permanent establishments.

On page 53, a pergola at Biltmore House, Biltmore,
North Carolina, and on pages 54 and 55 a view of
the Great Smokies from a balcony of Biltmore House.

At left, the Victorian mansion "Saluda," at Flat Rock, North Carolina. *Immediately below,* the spring house at Hickory Nut Gap Farm, North Carolina; *at bottom,* a slave house at Flat Rock.

Biltmore House is the greatest country house ever built
in North America. Designed by Richard Morris Hunt
for George W. Vanderbilt, it was begun in 1890 and
completed in 1895, when Vanderbilt was thirty. (He is
said to have asked for a simple shooting box; Hunt
knew better.) The park surrounding the house
originally comprised 125,000 acres; the house itself
contains four acres of floor space. Still in the possession
of the family, the house is open to the public.

Above, the conservatory, where Vanderbilt liked to be
served his after-dinner coffee.

Above, a stilt house at Nag's Head, a small community on the Outer Banks of North Carolina. Once accessible only by boat, this wild stretch of coast is now connected to the mainland by causeways; Cape Hatteras, scene of many shipwrecks, marks its farthest thrust into the Atlantic. Nag's Head is near Kitty Hawk, where, in 1903, the Wright Brothers made the first powered and controlled flight in history.

At right, the cast-iron stairway at "Saluda," in Flat Rock — a rural mansion bravely aspiring to urban grandeur.

The Grove Park Inn, in Asheville,
North Carolina, is the bizarre
brainchild of a millionaire
patent-medicine manufacturer named
Grove. Built in 1913, it became
one of the leading summer
resort hotels in the South.
The exterior looks as old as
Machu Picchu; the unaltered
interior might be 1978.

The Jersey Shore

Of all the regions on the North American continent that people have chosen to spend their summers in, none has been more popular over countless generations than the New Jersey shore. From Cape May, at the southernmost tip of the state, to the Atlantic Highlands, where the northern curve of the coast bends inward towards the kills and bays of New York harbor, scarcely a mile of beach goes unoccupied in summer. The resorts crowd upon and jostle one another, not without occasional disdain: Long Branch, Elberon, Deal, Asbury Park, Ocean Grove, Spring Lake, Atlantic City — each has its quiddity, though all share the same seemingly illimitable sweep of sea, the same burnished sky.

This coast has been frequented for so long that its assorted settlements amount to chapters in a textbook of architectural history, where the rise and fall of a succession of styles can be readily marked and studied. Just here one encounters an airy wooden "hygienic" cottage of the 1860s, all windows and porches, through which sea breezes blow upward to emerge from a cupola at the highest peak of the roof; there, one observes a row of immense white turn-of-the-century mansions, flung up along a broad seaside avenue within such close range of each other that a fastidious visitor, Henry James, compared them to a more or less monstrous string of pearls.

What is à la mode in architecture is as subject to change as what is à la mode in millinery. In the case of summer resorts, sometimes an entire community will go out of vogue and be preserved by neglect and poverty until, fifty or a hundred years later, it is restored to favor. Something like this has been the fortunate fate of Cape May, whose enchanting many-colored fretwork houses and hotels were once threatened with demolition and which now make up a national historic district, preserved forever from the fickle tyrannies of taste.

Residents of the Jersey shore have
rarely seemed to require much privacy.
Perhaps because so many of its summer
resorts began as religious camp-meetings
or chautauquas, people have long been
accustomed to being crowded together
in them. Besides, life in summer is lived
largely out-of-doors, on lawns and beaches
and in the sea itself, where numbers
provide a certain reassurance.

On the facing page are views of *(above)*
the boardwalk at Bay Head and *(below)*
the serried ranks of hotels at Spring Lake.

Above at left is a lone house at Spring
Lake. From the time of the Civil War
until the turn of the century, most of
the houses built along this coast could
have been designed by pastry chefs
instead of architects.

Below at left is a spun-sugar confection
at Cape May.

Above is the celebrated Margate elephant,
undergoing repairs. She is big enough to
live in and has proved more satisfactory
to generations of school children than
any living elephant could be.

The prettiest churches built in summer resorts in the nineteenth century were almost invariably Episcopalian; they were small and trim, with proud belfries and with such delightful (and ominous) names as "St. Mary in Peril of the Sea." When the peril proved real, the churches could usually be picked up and moved further inland.

On the facing page is St. Peter's-by-the-Sea, at Cape May Point, rising modestly heavenward. *Above,* the pre-Disneyland splendor of the much-added-onto Blenheim-Marlborough Hotel, facing the boardwalk at Atlantic City.

Long Island

Walt Whitman, who was born on Long Island, called it "fish-shaped Paumonak," and on a map one sees at once how its head seems to nuzzle the rocky shore of Manhattan, how its rounded whale's body separates Long Island Sound from the open sea, and how its tail divides into northerly and southerly flukes, with Shelter Island and a few lesser islands nestling cozily between them. Geologically, Long Island is a souvenir of the last Ice Age. It is the terminal moraine of the Wisconsin Glacier, which is to say that it consists of the heaped-up debris of gravel and boulders that the glacier had been pushing before it over innumerable centuries and then left behind in the course of its long retreat to the Arctic.

The north shore of Long Island is marked by high bluffs, dropping to a narrow shingle; the south shore is an almost unbroken succession of broad beaches, stretching a hundred and twenty-five miles from Coney Island to Montauk. Off the south shore is a wisp of sand and scrub some fifty miles in length and in many places but a few hundred yards across; this is Fire Island, to whose frail bosom cling a dozen small summer resorts, all in constant peril of the sea. But then the entire coastline of Long Island might be described in those terms, as sharing the same sunny prospects in summer, the same harsh and sometimes terrifying prospects in winter. The resorts range from what are little more than shanty colonies in Jamaica Bay to the great, many-chimneyed, shingled mansions of the Hamptons; and their implacable enemy is the sea, which, wracked by storms, hurls itself again and again on the readily breachable dunes. Houses that have been built hundreds of feet in from the assumed high water mark may find themselves in the course of a few years encircled by fierce tides; other houses will have been flung headlong into the surf and pounded to matchwood. Nevertheless, the houses go on being built, the rock-faced seawalls go on being repaired and strengthened, for it is in the nature of summer people not to be able to believe for long in the murderous energy of winter.

On pages 78-79, a leisurely weekend luncheon in East Hampton. Beyond the dunes lies the sea and beyond the sea lies Portugal. *At top of page,* the trees and hedges that make East Hampton seem an English village.

Below, the south shore of Long Island is a hundred-mile-long sequence of white beaches differing only in name and popularity.

On facing page, the interior of a fishing cottage at Montauk, designed in the eighties by McKim, Mead & White, who later took to designing palaces.

On the facing page, the Lamb house, East Hampton. Formerly the studio of the nineteenth-century landscape painter Thomas Moran, who would sketch all summer in the Far West and paint his vast canvases here and in New York all winter. *Below,* a house on the dunes. Sixty-five years ago, when it was built, a hundred feet of lawn stretched to the beach. If the dunes continue to wear away, the house will soon be swallowed up by the sea. *Above,* the ancient pond on the village green in East Hampton.

Nearly a hundred and fifty years ago, Coney Island was as popular a summer resort with New York society as East Hampton is today. It was only a short distance from the city by steamer or train and it boasted half a dozen fashionable hotels along its boardwalk. As the decades passed, the fickle rich went elsewhere and first the middle class and then the lower classes in all their teeming millions took over "Coney." For long it was one of the premier amusement parks in the country; today the Ferris wheel still turns, but the sea air seems peopled with ghosts and the boardwalk is filled with joggers.

The Berkshires

In the naming of mountains, the first white settlers generally took their cue from local Indian usage. The Appalachians as a whole and the separate ranges within the Appalachians – the Adirondacks, the Alleghenies, and the like – were given Indian names or such names as the Great Smokies and the Blue Ridge, which are said to be more or less accurate translations from Indian tongues. The Berkshires are an exception; they bear a name that was taken from the Old World and has nothing to do with their appearance or with the natives that lived among them. Still, the name is less inappropriate than it might have been; it evokes the tranquil English countryside, and the Berkshires are indeed so gentle in nature that, despite the height of a few of their peaks, they are rarely described as mountains. To most of their inhabitants, they are simply and modestly the Berkshire Hills.

Throughout the eighteenth and early nineteenth centuries, the Berkshires prospered from agriculture; crops flourished in the well-watered valleys and cattle and sheep grazed in the upland pastures. With the opening up of the West, agriculture declined, but in its place as a source of income arrived an ever-expanding host of summer people. Railroads brought the fashionable rich west from Boston and north from New York, and villages that had once served as markets for farmers – Stockbridge, Lenox, Great Barrington – found themselves waiting with profit upon the owners of newly created estates, many of which were on an immense scale. The closest that American country life at the turn of the century ever came to rivaling that of England was when houses of a hundred rooms and more were being built in the high green valleys of the Berkshires, amidst lawns and gardens and woods that seemed to stretch to the horizon. For a few weeks of the year, the big houses blazed with lights, and carriages came and went up and down the graveled drives under files of elms, bearing guests to and from innumerable dinner parties and balls; then, the summer people having departed, the houses went dark and the caretakers huddled dozing in the kitchen wing, waiting for the long, bitter winter to pass.

At right, the marquee over the entrance to "Wheatleigh," one of the surviving great houses in Lenox. A wealthy American girl having married an Italian nobleman, her father gave the young couple the present of a sumptuous villa in the Italian style. At the foot of the classical water tower are the gravestones of a score of poodles belonging to the late mistress of "Wheatleigh."

On pages 88-89, a garden in Lenox, Massachusetts.

Below, a playhouse, mostly for grown-ups, in Norfolk, Connecticut. Having abundant water power, Norfolk in the eighteenth century was a thriving industrial community. It then fell upon hard times and, like so many high, cold, stony, isolated New England villages, was rescued in the late nineteenth century by becoming a summer resort.

Near right, above: this window in a barn in Norfolk once gave light to the belfry of a chapel at Yale College. When the chapel was torn down, an alumnus of Yale, George Case, carried the window up to Norfolk and installed it in a building on his estate. His daughter having sold the estate took care that the window went with her.

Far right, above: windows at the Choate house in Stockbridge. It was designed in the eighties by McKim, Mead & White, who playfully mixed broken bottle glass with the mortar that binds the bricks above the arched windows; in the morning sun, the windows are outlined as if by blazing diamonds.

Below, the Chinese garden at the Choate house, seen from above.

Two examples of craftsmanship in wood at the
turn of the century. *Left*, the ceiling of a loggia
at "Wheatleigh," designed for ventilation as well
as beauty. *Below*, a shelter at Norfolk, serving
a golf course that long ago returned to forest.

"Yaddo" is a large country estate on the outskirts of Saratoga, built by Mr. and Mrs. Spencer Trask of New York City. After Trask's death, his widow endowed it as a retreat for artists, writers and composers. Novelists as unlike as Truman Capote and Philip Roth have contentedly shared the peace and quiet (to say nothing of the grandeur) of "Yaddo."

Saratoga began as a spa, but its popularity greatly increased when to hygiene were added the pleasures of gambling at Canfield's and betting at the racetrack. No matter where one turns at Saratoga, one encounters horses, even *(left)* on the carved rafters of the grandstand roof.

Right, the finish line. To the true bettor, the beauty of the track and the beauty of the day go unnoticed; the horse one has bet on is all.,

The North Woods

That great portion of the Appalachian range which embraces the Catskills and the Adirondacks in New York State and the White and Green Mountains in New Hampshire and Vermont is many millions of acres in extent – a crumpled highland threaded with innumerable lakes and rivers and much of it more densely forested today than it was a hundred years ago. The forest takes us by surprise; indeed, our first thought as we enter these mountains is that, close as they are to New York City, Boston, and other populous areas, they give the impression of being almost as impenetrable to us as they were to the earliest explorers and settlers. Those gallant pioneers were quickly followed by fishermen and hunters, for no sooner does man succeed with painful efforts in taming nature than he casts about for some means of enjoying it in a wholly untamed form. The city rich in their big, chock-a-block houses are always especially quick to give way to this seduction. In the 1860s and 1870s, they began by visiting one or another of the immense wooden hotels built for their pleasure on the shores of mountain lakes or perched in the cleft of some high mountain pass; then they began to put up their own formidable dwellings, big enough to shelter not only a family and its friends but an attendant army of servants.

The celebrated Adirondack camps of wealthy New Yorkers – the Vanderbilts, Morgans, Whitneys, and the rest – are a product of this period. The camps were the inspiration of a gifted young amateur architect and entrepreneur named William West Durant. The camps looked as primitive as they were pretty, but they took care to contain every imaginable luxury; one dined as well at them as on Fifth Avenue. When the camps were built, they were accessible by train, lake steamer, and buckboard wagon; in 1978, the few remaining camps are accessible only by car. The trains, steamers, and buckboards have vanished without a trace, save at the Adirondack Museum, overlooking Blue Mountain Lake, where Harold K. Hochschild, the preeminent historian of the region, has preserved a few choice specimens.

Below, a cabin at "Pine Knot," on Raquette Lake.
Designed and built by William West Durant, "Pine Knot"
(the Victorians had a weakness for puns) was eventually
sold to the railroad magnate Collis P. Huntington.

At right, from top to bottom,
a stone barn at Kamp Kill Kare, a bay window at "Pine Knot,"
and a woodshed at Kamp Kill Kare.

At left, the interior of one of the cabins at "Pine Knot." Durant made use of whatever materials could be gathered from the surrounding forest (including raccoon skulls) to decorate the walls and ceilings of the dozen or so buildings at "Pine Knot." The furniture, too, was composed of local wood, leather, and horns.

On the facing page, a well-aired fire hose, a leaded-glass door at Kamp Kill Kare, an Adirondacks stool, and a few keepsake silhouettes of species of fish that were caught in nearby waters.

Overleaf, a classic mountain railroad station; this one is at North Conway, New Hampshire.

Facing page
A bridge over the inlet leading
to Eagle Lake, near the town of
Blue Mountain Lake. The bridge
was designed and built by
William West Durant, in 1891,
as a memorial to his father,
Dr. Thomas C. Durant.

At top
The main lodge at Kamp Kill Kare.
Most Adirondacks camps consist
of a village-like scattering of
buildings, accumulated over the
years and having this advantage:
in case of fire, an entire camp
is unlikely to be destroyed.

Above left
A homemade fire engine at Kamp
Kill Kare. *Above right,* interior
of a camp at Canada Lake.
Overleaf
Mohonk House, in the Shawangunk
Mountains, for over a hundred
years a popular summer hotel.

A nineteenth-century marvel, the
Mount Washington Cog Railway is
three and a third miles long, rising
by a grade of one foot in three to a
height of 6,284 feet. A cog road of
the rack and pinion type, with
ratchets that prevent the wheels
from slipping backward, it was the
first of its kind in the world and has
been in operation every summer
since 1869.

Now at the Adirondack Museum,
in Blue Mountain Lake, this private
railroad car was built by the
Pullman Company in 1889–1890, at
a cost of $60,000, for Austin
Corbin, President of the Long
Island Railway Company. Later, it
was used by August Belmont,
President of the Louisville &
Nashville Railroad Company, and
by his successor Henry Walters.

The New England Coast

One thinks at first of the lines by Felicia Hemans, faithfully memorized by every nineteenth-century schoolchild—"The breaking waves dashed high / On a stern and rock-bound coast"—and it is certainly the case that the rocks are there, from the low granite parapets of the Connecticut and Rhode Island shores to the fortress-like heights of Mount Desert, in Maine. But then one remembers so much smiling sand as well: the seemingly endless stretches of it that make up the coiled sea-serpent of Cape Cod, the many small coves in which, at the foot of heaped-up, sheltering boulders, a half-circle of gently sloping beach invites the paddler, the clammer, the swimmer, the supine sun-worshipper. It is a coast that in the storms of winter leads one to suppose that it must be uninhabitable; in the benignities of July and August, look! there is a face at every window.

More than anywhere else on the continent, the history of the towns along this coast can be traced by strangers; their direct lines of descent from port to resort are as visible as their piers and wharves, their rusting bollards and old lobster boats sinking in green muck. Saybrook, Stonington, New London, Newport, New Bedford, Martha's Vineyard, Nantucket, Chatham, Wellfleet, Provincetown, Gloucester, Portsmouth, Kennebunkport, Camden, North Haven, Machias—in and out of their snug harbors sailed fleets of ships bent upon money-making in the four quarters of the globe: whaling ships, ships in the China trade, ships in trade with the West Indies, ships carrying ice to Brazil, or guano back from Peru. When, for whatever reason, the trade eventually failed and the ports languished, little by little in the place of sailors and merchant-captains and a dolorous plenty of black-shawled widows came the first summer people. The sea for them was a place to play upon, not wrest a living from; every morning from their newly remodeled old houses they looked out to sea, but what they saw wasn't what the builders of the houses had seen: under the least chuckling sunstruck wavelet a drowned man floating.

The parvenu grandees of Newport vied with each other in the opulence and variety of the immense "cottages" they built. *Above,* two garden walls in different styles aggressively collide, each pretending that its neighbor doesn't exist. *At left,* the Casino at Newport was designed by McKim, Mead & White, in 1879, at the prompting of the irascible publisher and society figure James Gordon Bennett, Jr., who is said to have been denied a renewal of his membership in the Reading Room. The Casino is an early example of mixed-use architecture: retail shops face the street on the ground floor, while the private activities of the Casino are reserved for the garden front and the upper floors. Several Japanese buildings had been erected at the Centennial Exposition in Philadelphia, in 1876; the Casino reflects a strong Japanese influence.

McKim, Mead & White went from designing pleasant summer houses in the shingle
style to designing palaces of limestone
and marble; "Rosecliff" was built for
a newly rich family that hoped to feel at
home in a seaside Versailles. Today,
tourists glance out over the Cliff Walk
to an assortment of houses that are,
in most cases, still in private hands.

Top, a garden at Manchester-by-the-Sea. The very difficulty of establishing a garden on a rocky coast drenched in salt air has sufficed to give pleasure to generations of rigid New Englanders. *Below,* a house that adventurously celebrates craftsmanship in wood, in a style that soon gave way to neo-Tudor, neo-Renaissance, and neo-Georgian pastiches.

Facing page, top, at Nahant, on the north shore of Massachusetts, a verandah whose stained-glass doors slide open and shut on a melodrama of continuously changing weather. *Below,* a cottage at Oak Bluffs, on Martha's Vineyard, once a popular Methodist campground. The tiny cottages were frowned on by some as being too worldly for Methodism.

Facing page, a cottage on the rocky coast at Kennebunkport, Maine.
Above, a house in the shape of a ship, perched as if in dry-dock at North Haven, Maine. The framing, inside and out, displays the ingenuity of ships' carpenters of an earlier day; no less ingenious is the contemporary chimney stack in the galley. *Overleaf,* Northeast Harbor, on Mount Desert Island.

Jeannette's beach, North Haven, Maine

The Maritimes

The coasts of Newfoundland and Labrador were well known to fleets of European fishermen long before the mainland of North America began to be explored and settled in the fifteenth and sixteenth centuries. (In recent years, it has become increasingly plain that commerce between the Old World and the New flourished continuously for perhaps a thousand years before Columbus made his celebrated "discovery" among the islands to the south.) The great French sea captain Jacques Cartier entered what was later to be known as the Gulf of the St. Lawrence in 1534 and the following year began to explore the shorelines of the river proper, finding evidence that Spanish adventurers had been there before him, presumably seeking gold. Cartier entered a bay on the river on August 10, 1535, naming it after a Spanish-born Saint Lawrence whose feast day it was. Over the years, the name that Cartier bestowed on the bay came to be applied to the entire river.

The Maritime Provinces—New Brunswick, Nova Scotia, and Prince Edward Island—are in their political structure an invention of the nineteenth century. For many generations, the welfare of the Maritimes depended on an economy of "wood, wind, and water"; only water, with its fishing industry, has proved of lasting good. More and more as the years have passed, the Maritimes have come to depend for survival upon their natural beauty, which attracts innumerable tourists and summer residents.

The rugged little Canadian island of Campobello is separated from the United States by scarcely more than a tide-rip and, since 1962, has been connected to the States by the Roosevelt International Bridge. It is the site of the only international park in the world—the Roosevelt Campobello Park, named in honor of President Franklin D. Roosevelt, who first came to Campobello in 1883, as a year-old infant, shortly after the island began to be frequented by American summer residents. Elizabeth, the Queen Mother, opened the Park Center in 1967 with the words, "It is most fitting that the memory of so gallant and industrious an American should be honored on the Canadian island which he loved." The Park contains upwards of three thousand acres; its focal point is the Roosevelt cottage, *above.*

Right, an interior view of the cottage. Roosevelt had a certain gift for architecture, but when it came to interior decoration, whether at his home at Hyde Park or on Campobello, chance accumulation and homely comfort were obviously the criteria.

Facing page, above, a bedroom in the Roosevelt cottage; below, the annunciator board in the servants' quarters. (No matter how simple and rustic the life led by the rich in summer, it took plenty of servants to keep it functioning.) Above, a view from the nearby Hubbard cottage.

The five Roosevelt children were brought up on Campobello, much as F.D.R. himself had been — to sail, swim, fish, and play games in the strenuous style favored by the family over many generations.

At thirty-nine, Roosevelt was stricken with polio on Campobello. He was carried off the island on a stretcher in September, 1921, to begin the long years of struggle, both physical and political, that led him to the Presidency. He didn't return to Campobello until June, 1933, four months after taking office, when he sailed into Welshpool Harbor at the helm of Amberjack II.

Above, a child's playhouse at
St. Andrews, New Brunswick, and,
left, the Algonquin Hotel at St. Andrews.
The town, located on a promontory
jutting out into Passamaquoddy Bay,
was founded by American Loyalists
who, at the time of the Revolution,
chose the Crown over independence.
British Army engineers laid out the
town and the first settlers arrived
from Maine in 1783. The cross-streets
of the town were named after George III
and his twelve children; a less fecund
monarch might have caused the engineers
some nomenclatural difficulties. During
its early years, St. Andrews was a
prosperous port, trading with the West
Indies and, thanks to the great forests
of New Brunswick, furnishing masts
and spars for the British Navy. The
town's prosperity was declining when,
at the turn of the twentieth century,
it became a fashionable summer resort.
The Canadian Pacific Railway built
the Algonquin Hotel and many exe-
cutives of the railway erected summer
homes in the vicinity. Today, St.
Andrews is also an important center
for marine biological research.

The pleasing summer houses of St. Andrews reflect the best aspects of the arts-and-crafts movement that flourished in Great Britain and Canada before the First World War; the built-in furniture and airy openness of the rooms are typical of the period. St. Andrews takes pride in its world-famous tides, which have an average rise and fall of twenty-eight feet. The community is also proud of its stability: almost fifty per cent of the houses are over a hundred years old and many are almost two hundred years old.

Above, the Thinkers' Lodge at Pugwash, Nova
Scotia. The celebrated American industrialist Cyrus
Eaton was born on the family farm at Pugwash
ninety-six years ago. In 1957, he began at Pugwash
a series of conferences, chaired by Bertrand Russell,
that drew politicians and philosophers from all over
the world. Skeptics spoke darkly of "hogwash from
Pugwash," but the world listened.

Facing page, above, exterior of the summer home
of the railroad magnate Sir William Van Horne
on Ministers Island, St. Andrews, New Brunswick;
below, the dining room.

Alexander Graham Bell was born in Edinburgh in 1847, came to Canada in 1870, and a few years later, while working with deaf students in Boston, invented the telephone. Having struck it rich, he and his family purchased a summer place at Baddeck, on Cape Breton Island, Nova Scotia. Bell himself designed their first house, "The Lodge," making a little cardboard model of it for the builders to emulate.

In the nineties, Bell built a far bigger house, "Beinn Breagh," which is Gaelic for "beautiful mountain." Gradually, it grew from a substantial summer estate into a kingdom, over which Bell, with his white beard, homespun knickerbockers, and old black tam-o'-shanter, presided with a child's relish. He was a happy egotist, testing his mettle in a score of endeavors, from publishing to powered flight.

Prince Edward Island boasts of
being the smallest province in
Canada and of having the warmest
ocean bathing. The lighthouse
above has slipped its moorings; no
longer needed as a warning beacon,
it has been carried inland and made
over into a cozy summer house.

Not all beachcombers live in the South Seas. Even in the comparatively cold climate of Canada, people walk the beaches seeking such treasures as shells, stones, and driftwood — also such leavings of the sea as will serve to create a patchwork quilt of a squatter's shack.

The St. Lawrence

Back in the nineties, a historian living on the banks of the St. Lawrence set impassioned pen to paper, hoping to call attention to what he rightly regarded as one of the natural wonders of the world. We may smile at his high-flown verbiage, yet much of it remains, in 1978, uncannily apt:

"There is in North America a mighty river [that] rises in the great fresh-water sea and ends in the great Atlantic — in places ten miles wide, at others less than a mile . . . . It runs for very many miles between two great nations — a river as grand as the La Plata, as picturesque as the Rhine, as pure as the lakes of Switzerland. Need we say that this wonderful stream is the St. Lawrence, the noblest, purest, most enchanting river of all God's beautiful earth? This noble stream drains nearly the whole of that vast region lying between the 41st and 49th degrees of north latitude and the 60th and 93rd parallels of longitude. Why this noble river is not more generally known is perhaps accounted for in part by the fact that it traverses a region of the country remote from the great thoroughfares of the world's commerce and trade. It lies along the boundary line of business. Its banks, to be sure, are dotted here and there with thriving towns and cities, several of considerable importance in the world's traffic, but its grand use is in connecting the great lakes with the ocean. . . . Its picturesque windings, pure water, wonderful atmosphere, and great and varied beauty of scenery are witnessed in such wonderful and lavish profusion nowhere else."

A hotel in Murray Bay, on the north shore of the St. Lawrence. The first summer hotels in this vicinity, built in the eighties, were scarcely larger than private houses; as the area prospered, the hotels increased in size, being continuously added onto until, at a distance, with their variety of gables and towers, they appeared to be ample villages in themselves.

Facing page, a view of Murray Bay,
described by its champions in the
early 1920s as "the Newport of
Canada [where] wealth, fashion,
youth, and beauty hold high carnival
in the beauteous Laurentian hills." In
those days, horse-drawn carriages
were still in vogue and the automobile
was considered a recent and
lamentable intrusion. Bright red
roofs — the one above crowns a house
in Rivière du Loup — are characteristic
of the locality.

Facing page
Two ample, unpretentious summer places in Murray Bay. Unlike Newport, Murray Bay has never sought to make a loud noise in the world. It prefers old money to new, and while it may be the case that, as the saying goes, money talks, it is also the case that old money has a tendency to whisper.

Two Gothic structures in Tadoussac, a town at the mouth of the tumultuous Saguenay River. (The upper structure is a summer church, the lower is a laundry.) Tadoussac has been a summer resort since Indian days. Great numbers of European fishermen anchored off Tadoussac in the sixteenth century and here the French made their first formal settlement in the New World.

Along the great river in summer, in whatever town or village, three things are sure to be readily visible: a church spire, a fishing pole, a garden. Priests have been saying Mass in French-speaking Canada for almost four centuries; the cross entered the wilderness along with the axe. Glancing over a map of the region, one guesses that certain place-names were the handiwork of priests, minds fixed on heaven (the town of Notre Dame du Portage, pictured immediately above, is surely an example), while others were the handiwork of trappers, whose imaginations took an earthier turn. (Tadoussac is said to be named for the mountains that rise above the town; a bowdlerized English version of the Montagnais original would be "rounded summits.")

The Thousand Islands

Early French explorers named the islands "*Les Mille Isles*," presumably for reasons of euphony and not arithmetic, since there are, in fact, something over fifteen hundred islands in the archipelago, ranging in area from a few square feet of rocks to islands containing thousands of acres of fields and woods. The boundary between the United States and Canada passes in a series of easy loops among the islands, for the most part following the main channel of the St. Lawrence. Until late in the nineteenth century, all the land on the American side of the boundary was owned by a single real estate promotion company, which, operating out of Alexandria Bay, energetically turned the region into a fashionable summer resort. At its most fashionable, around the turn of the century, this region threatened to rival Newport in the fancy of the rich; scores of steam yachts were to be seen cruising among the islands, brightly striped awnings stretched above their fantails, Oriental rugs on their teak decks, and, at night, Japanese lanterns blooming like many-colored moons from their masts and rigging. As at Newport, shingled cottages tended to give way to immense mansions in stone and slate; most of these mansions have since fallen into decay, or have been thrown down, while the proud little turreted wooden cottages continue to assert their presence at the water's edge.

The great shingled boathouses that were built to shelter the assorted
boating craft of Boldt Castle, at Alexandria Bay, are architecturally
more interesting than the famous old unfinished castle itself.
(The wife of the millionaire who was building the castle unexpectedly
died, and he is said to have been too bereft to complete it.)

Below, a view of gargoyles guarding Cherry Island and two views of Bourne Castle, on Dark Island, whose walls frown convincingly on strangers.

Above
A sight that has become common on
the river and yet remains as hard to
believe as any mirage: against the
low, wooded skyline, an enormous
tanker will suddenly appear, seeming
to split whole islands in two as
it makes its relentless progress up
or down river.

Left
A St. Lawrence River rowing skiff,
a light-weight craft designed for
carrying out easy excursions among
the islands.

Facing page
The entrance hall to Bourne Castle;
stern medievalism quickly gives
way to sunny rooms and terraces.

Every island seems its own contentedly separate kingdom, boasting a castle or a cottage and boathouses whether large or small and with pockets of gardens flourishing unexpectedly in the ledges along the shore. The means of transportation among the kingdoms is, of course, boats—boats by the hundreds, in every size and shape, lovingly varnished and polished and coddled into extreme old age.

Ontario: The Northern Lakes

The high, rocky tableland a hundred miles north of Toronto is filled with lakes remarkable for their number, their size, their depth, and their beauty. The three linked lakes of Muskoka, Rosseau, and Joseph have been popular summer resorts for upwards of a hundred years; along their shores and on their uncounted hundreds of wooded islands summer residents not only from throughout Canada but from the States as well have built cottages (and boathouses as big as cottages) in a score of styles, each favored by a generation and then passed over with, at best, affectionate mockery by the generations that follow. What the styles have in common is that they are all based on wood; inside and out, they manifest the playful imaginations and exceptional manual skills of local artisans, working on occasion from blueprints but more often from what seemed to them, in a certain green pocket of hitherto untouched wilderness, a pleasing form for a summer house to take.

On pages 164–165, a panoramic view
of Lake Joseph. Sunlight burns on
the water with a Mediterranean
brilliance, but in the evergreen woods
the air has an upland coolness. *Above,*
an over-sized "mother" boathouse
appears to have given birth to a
contented, nuzzling child.

A proud litter of launches in the locks
at Port Carling, on the Indian River.
The river leads from Lake Rosseau into
Lake Muskoka, which is at an
elevation four feet lower than
Rosseau; the locks in summer provide
a not unwelcome traffic jam of
dazzling craft and well-tanned
mariners.

In the nineteenth century, architects took as much pleasure in designing the dependencies of a house—stables, water towers, boathouses, gazebos—as in designing the house itself. *Left,* a boathouse at Muskoka that has something of the look of a medieval reliquary; *facing page,* also at Muskoka, a water tower, the lower floors of which serve as a laundry room and sheltered drying yard. (The first master of the house objected to the sight of his undergarments drying *en plein air.*) In the early days, water had to be pumped out of the lake by steam engine into a high tank, from which it would descend by gravity through a labyrinth of pipes inside the house and out. A great deal of water went to irrigate gardens, in which much-needed vegetables as well as flowers were grown.

On pages 170-171, a youth campsite at Lake Timagami. Though many girls and boys acquire a taste for roughing it at these camps, as they grow older most of them come to prefer a certain measure of domestic comfort—a familiar bedroom to wake up in, windows open onto a familiar lawn, and perhaps the sound of someone already busily astir belowstairs. Lying half asleep under the bedclothes, one waits for the first delectable odors of coffee and bacon to come drifting up through the painted floorboards.

Of the innumerable rocky islands
lying scattered throughout the vastness
of Georgian Bay, in Lake Huron, many
are best reached by amphibian plane.

Much of Georgian Bay remains a
wilderness. One could pitch a tent
there in summer and live a life not
much different from that lived by
the local Indians four centuries ago.

Muskoka is another story; it has
been a tamed wilderness for
generations. If one is wakened in
the early morning by the sound
of something thudding heavily
on wood, it is likely not to be a
beaver but a boy in a speedboat,
hurling a daily paper onto the dock.

Michigan

In the Middle West, more than in any other part of the country, the founding of summer resorts during the last quarter of the nineteenth century was often associated with religion. Many of the villages that sprang up along the shores of the Great Lakes and hundreds of smaller lakes served at first as campgrounds for Methodists or sites of Chautauqua assemblies; the intention of their founders was to combine wholesome outdoor living with the worship of God and the education of man. Temperance became an affiliated interest, as, afterwards, did women's suffrage. In the fashionable resorts to the east, women reigned as society figures, their husbands tagging along to pay the bills and sit more or less uncomfortably at the head of the table (a leading artist of the period, Charles Dana Gibson, never tired of drawing the American husband as a victim of his tyrannical, social-climbing wife). In the Middle West, women and men worked together more nearly as equals, especially where good causes were concerned; the seductions of Society, with its excluding capital "S," were to come later, when the religious impetus diminished and competition on many levels — sports, party-giving, conspicuous display — became the measure not of one's happiness but of one's success. In the fierce struggle to dominate Newport or Bar Harbor, nobody had ever expected the contestants to be happy; in the Middle West, it had remained for long the most natural of goals. With the change, the holy simplicity that had hovered in groves and tabernacles vanished, and with few mourners, for the grand chase of the twentieth century would have other beasts in view.

Back in the 1840s,
William Cullen Bryant predicted
that it would be the fate
of Mackinac Island to become
a popular watering place.
"Its climate during the summer
months is delightful,"
he wrote. "There is no air
more pure and elastic,
and the winds of the south and
southwest, which are so
hot on the prairies, arrive here
tempered to a grateful
coolness by the waters over
which they have swept...
I cannot but think with a kind
of regret on the time which,
I suppose, is near at hand, when
its wild and lonely woods
will be intersected with highways
and filled with cottages
and boarding houses."
Bryant's prediction came true;
the cottages he feared are by
now nearly a hundred years
old and are rightly cherished by
their owners. This splendid
stairway in a Mackinac cottage
shows that local carpenters
early learned to execute joinery
of the highest quality.

Over the years, the breezy open
porch of Victorian times had a
tendency to become absorbed into
the house proper, first by the
addition of screening and then by
being glassed in. By the twenties, it
was commonly known as a
sunroom, serving in practice as a
second living room; later, it would
be the favored setting for TV.

On pages 182-183, *at top,* four cottages on the West Bluff at Mackinac Island, built in the nineties by wealthy midwesterners. *Below,* the Grand Hotel on Mackinac Island.

Opened in 1887, it was—and is—one of the largest summer hotels in the world; its front verandah is 800 feet long. In the nineties, a guest at the hotel wrote, "We found the guest rooms large, airy, and elegantly furnished. The elevators and call bells placed us in easy reach of the office and the electric lights and gas were quite metropolitan. The rooms were offered us at $3 and $5 per day."

Left, view from the verandah of the Grand Hotel and, *below,* some nineteenth-century vehicles (including an Irish tub cart) that are still happily in use, private cars being forbidden.

The Rockies

Traveling through the Canadian West in 1913, the English poet Rupert Brooke was made uneasy by the fact that the mountains, though beautiful, gave so few signs of human occupation. "Here one is perpetually a first-comer," he wrote. "The land is virginal, the wind cleaner than elsewhere, and every lake new-born, and each day is the first day. The flowers are less conscious than English flowers, the breezes have nothing to remember and everything to promise. There walk, as yet, no ghosts of lovers in Canadian lanes. This is the essence of the gray freshness and brisk melancholy of this land. And for all the charm of those qualities, it is also the secret of the European's discontent. For it is possible, at a pinch, to do without gods. But one misses the dead." Brooke might have felt more comfortable in the American Rockies, which have an ample supply of ghosts — ghosts of innumerable Indian, American, English, French, and Spanish warriors, hunters, fishermen, and explorers. Once the Indians with much bloodshed had been driven off their lands, the first ranches were able to come into existence; long after them came the so-called "dude" ranches and then the ranches occupied as summer homes. Now the West, sparsely populated as it is, begins to fear overcrowding, for its essence is a superb, self-chosen isolation; a neighbor is near enough who lives in the next valley.

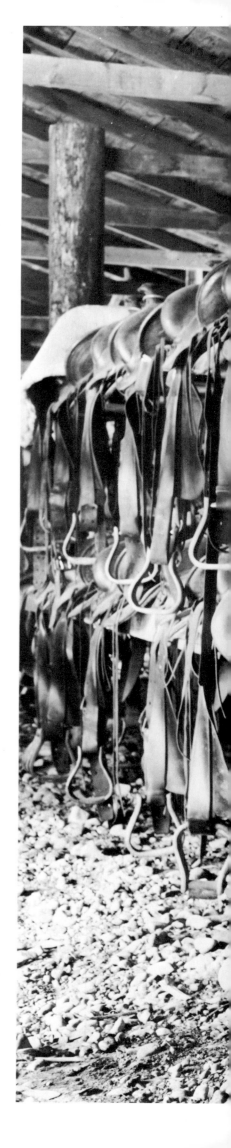

Probably the simplest summer living is to be found on
a ranch, where the limits of work and play are set not
by men but by horses. One spends the day in the saddle,
viewing the world from a height, and at nightfall returns
with reluctance to the world of the person on foot.

The Stanley Hotel in Estes Park, Colorado, built by
the inventor of the Stanley Steamer. *Below,* the geyser
Old Faithful, in Yellowstone National Park, Wyoming,
and the Old Faithful Inn, opened in 1904, "the largest
native-log structure in the Rocky Mountains." At inter-
vals of about sixty-five minutes, Old Faithful hurls some
fifteen thousand gallons of water a hundred and forty
feet into the air. Yellowstone is the first (1872)
and largest (3,472 square miles) U.S. national park.

Facing page, timber and sod remain
valued building materials throughout the West,
just as they were in Indian days.

Above, Banff Springs Hotel set against
the splendor of Mount Rundle.

On pages 194-195, interiors of the Old Faithful Inn
in the American Rockies and the Banff Springs
Hotel in the Canadian Rockies. The Canadian
Pacific Railway magnate Sir William Van Horne
sited the Banff Springs Hotel to take advantage
of what he called "the million-dollar view."

British Columbia

Although the region that in 1871 would become the Province of British Columbia was one of the last on the continent to be explored and settled by white men, it had long boasted a prosperous Indian culture; it was the land of the so-called potlatch people, celebrated for their bestowal, on ceremonial occasions, of extravagant gifts of food, cloth, and jewelry. The Spanish explored the coast in 1774, followed by Captain James Cook and Captain George Vancouver, both of His Majesty's Royal Navy. The first settlers traded in fur, and the region grew slowly in population until the great gold strike of 1858 and the arrival on the West Coast, in 1885, of the Canadian Pacific Railway. Three-quarters of the enormous area of the province lies at an elevation of at least three thousand feet above sea level; the Japanese Current warms the long, much-indented coast, and the climate of the southwest portion of the province is said to be one of the most favorable in the world for men, animals, and plants. Old folk bent on retirement tend to cluster there, while young folk bent on making their fortunes risk the more rugged climate and landscape to the north. At present, the population is less than fifty per cent British; among the ethnic groups represented in considerable numbers are the Dutch, the Germans, the Italians, the Chinese, the Japanese, the Swedes, and the Norwegians. The native Indian population has shrunk from perhaps a hundred thousand in 1800 to less than half that number today. Ironically, the descendants of the generous potlatch people live for the most part in extreme poverty; their ancient civilization makes no easy connection with the bustling contemporary world.

Above
The marina at Fisherman Cove, in West Vancouver, where the mountains tumble headlong into the Strait of Georgia. Sailing and fishing are among the chief sports activities of the region, whose communities are better served by innumerable ferry routes than by highways.

Facing page
Bowen Island, at the entrance to Howe Sound, consists of twenty square miles of rain forest, guarded by high bluffs; summer residents began to build here in Victorian times, turning what had been meager farmland into green lawns and brightly colored gardens.

The view from Bowen Island looks across the Strait of Georgia to Vancouver Island, on whose southern tip lies Victoria, capital city of British Columbia. The Strait carries a heavy traffic of tankers and freighters, Vancouver City being the largest Canadian port on the Pacific.

Left, the rain forest on Vancouver Island. The Pacific Rim Trail, which runs through the forest, is a favorite with hikers.

Top, a classic specimen of summer cabin; whether built on a mountain lake or along the coast, such a cabin will have a stone fireplace and a deck with a view and it will give the impression that if you were to lock it up and go away, in thirty years you would be able to return and find everything just as you had left it.
Directly above, a tiny but proudly decorated cedar shack.

A dwelling known as a float house,
which has the advantage of requiring
no ownership of land. Among its
disadvantages is that, unlike a
houseboat, it cannot be navigated;
its only journeys are vertical
ones, up and down with the tide.

A spectacular setting at Point No Point,
on Vancouver Island. The name was bestowed on
the point by a bygone surveyor with a wry
sense of humor. The Island looks out over
Juan de Fuca Strait to the heights of Olympic
National Park, in the state of Washington.

California

Everything that can be said about California sounds as if it were being shouted by a Chamber of Commerce booster at the top of his voice. Exceeded in size only by Alaska and Texas, California is the most populous state in the Union, the richest agricultural state, and the state whose per capita income is greater than that of any foreign nation. Its climate is so varied as to be both intensely dry and intensely wet; in some places, the temperature is as high as the Sahara, in others it is Arctically low. Wherever one lives, one is likely to be implicated in a superlative. Death Valley, two hundred and eighty-two feet below sea level, is the lowest point in the United States; a few miles away rises Mount Whitney, over fourteen thousand feet high and the second-highest point in the country (Mount McKinley, in Alaska, is the highest). California's Sierra Nevada mountains are higher than the Rockies; in them nestles Lake Tahoe, two hundred square miles in area and sixteen hundred feet deep. California offers the unpeopled wilderness of the Big Sur, looking out over the Pacific, and the jostling gregariousness of Chinatown, in San Francisco. In California, one can drive for as much as six hundred miles along a series of freeways without encountering a single stoplight. One can also walk through a forest of ancient redwoods or along miles of empty beach. California is famous for its radically eccentric religious sects, its superlative wines, its ghost towns (Bodie), its poverty (Watts), its opulence (San Simeon), its grass fires, its flash floods, its nudists, its poets, and its movie and TV stars. California wears a gold hat and it kicks high and as a compendium of improbable contrarieties it proves, not to its own surprise, irresistible.

"Wyntoon" was a favorite summer retreat of the publisher William Randolph Hearst and, before him, of his mother, Phoebe Apperson Hearst. At the turn of the century, Mrs. Hearst, who had a bent for architecture, commissioned Bernard Maybeck to build her a romantic Rhenish castle on the McCloud River, in Northern California. Later, when the castle burned, her son commissioned his favorite architect, Julia Morgan, to create what amounted to a sort of grown-up Hansel and Gretel village on the same site. The murals are by a fashionable artist of the twenties, Willy Pogany.

California contains hundreds of little rural health resorts,
which in most cases have grown up around mineral
springs reputed to possess exceptional curative powers.
Below, Walters Spring, in Napa County, and the
register of a nineteenth-century spa, frequented in
summer by wealthy visitors from San Francisco.

"Vikingsholm," or "Viking's House," on Emerald Bay,
Lake Tahoe. Designed by Lennart Palme and completed in 1929,
it was the summer residence of Mrs. Lora J. Knight,
of Santa Barbara, until her death in 1945. Mrs. Knight
wished the house, now open to the public, to
resemble as closely as possible a medieval Norse fortress.

A view on the McCloud River, whose swift waters are fed by the melting glacier of Mount Shasta; the river is a favored habitat of the Dolly Varden trout. The fish is named for a character in Dickens' *Barnaby Rudge,* who wore scarves covered with cherry-colored dots. Dolly Varden (*Salvelinus malma*) wears dots of many colors on its greenish back.

Facing page, left, the house at Soda Springs, where Mark Hopkins and his family often spent the summer. *Right,* a natural swimming hole on the north branch of the American River, in Soda Springs. Mark Twain, who was one of the few nineteenth-century Americans known to have enjoyed skinny-dipping, may have skinny-dipped here.

Beaches challenge us to make something out of nothing, or almost nothing: sea wrack, horseshoe crab shells, pebbles, the limitless sand itself. Curiously, western beaches seem to offer a greater challenge than eastern ones; more things on a large scale are to be encountered along the Pacific than along the Atlantic. Whether sand castles or driftwood sculpture, the purpose of these inventions is to be playful and make us smile; they also serve to lessen the terror we may feel from time to time in the presence of the immense emptiness of sea and sky. We need then to be reassured by something man-made; walking the crinkled waves' edge, we are grateful for the signature of our footsteps in the wet sand behind us.

Epilogue

Memories of summer places — how little prompting it takes to fetch them up out of the sun-dappled, brimming well of the past! And though at first we may pretend that these memories accurately reflect events that occurred in a certain place and at a certain time, it is not so; for the past isn't immutable simply because it is the past. On the contrary, it is subject to constant change: we manipulate it according to our needs, molding it into a shape that comes as close as possible to our heart's desire. Tirelessly prowling the years of our lives, as the old King of the Wood circled all night the sacred oak at Nemi, we cannot leave even the happiest of our memories untampered with.

The past isn't only what we spring from but what we are nourished by, and what gives us nourishment is bound to alter as we alter. By now, I find (occasionally to my discomfiture) that my memories of the past embrace other people's memories as well and that I cannot clearly distinguish one from the other. Words I've read, pictures I've seen, scraps of family gossip I've overheard — all feed the simple-seeming, infinitely complex stream of recollection into which, from time to time, I step for strength. The summer places of my youth have become a palimpsest of many summer places, spanning many decades. The Gulf Coast as I view it today is also the Gulf Coast of eighty-odd years ago, as Kate Chopin wrote about it in *The Awakening*. The sunny aberration of Biltmore House, gazing with Renaissance eyes out upon the Great Smokies, is hallowed for me because of the presence in it, once upon a time, of Henry James. His corpulent ghost paces the terrace of Biltmore House as it paces the terrace of Edith Wharton's house in Lenox and the cliff-walk at Newport. Similarly, I am with Hawthorne and Melville in the Berkshires, with Emerson in the Adirondacks, with Sarah Orne Jewett in Maine, and with Mark Twain in California. Their memories are my memories and I am wise in making no effort to disentangle them.

Firm as the bond is between words and memories, firmer still is the bond between pictures and memories. When we speak figuratively of looking back, isn't it the case that we are also literally looking back, as the phrase "in the mind's eye" implies? For our minds are not so much libraries as picture galleries; what we sift through in seeking out the past are innumerable likenesses of people, places, and things. It is only with difficulty that we can bring back the voices of friends and lovers, parents and children; conversations, however precious they may be, tend to reduce themselves in memory to a mere muddle of sound, blurred by affection or anger (the fiercer the emotion, the less we listen to what is being said). But pictures! They never lose their morning freshness; their immediacy can be like a blow in the face, a scalding of the heart, a balm. They are fixed forever and in them we are immortally young, immortally full of promise. We hug them to us; they are who we were and who we hope we are. The sun shines in them, making us squint, and the rain (for even in summer places there is rain, and sometimes a cold fog rolls in out of Erewhon) runs helter-skelter down the glistening pane and we hold out our hands to dear summer companions and feel their hands in ours.

Index of Photographs

NOTE: Photographs are listed in order of appearance, running from left to right.